Elena Pankey

CONTENTS

ISBN: 978-1-952907-94-4

Introduction

The book "Calendar 2026 & Stories. Peter the Rooster & His 7 Hens" is good for any family events and reading.
It has 12 month of the Calendar for 2026.

Also, it holds the real stories, which were observed through the security camera in the chicken coop.

The Rooster Peter cared deeply for his family, searching for food and protecting them.

Every day, the hens sang their tender songs and laid delicious eggs. They all believed that their destiny was to serve people.

January 2026

January, 2026

"The chickens have come home to roost"

Sun	Mon	Tue	Wed	Thu	Fri	Sat
				1	2	3
4	5	6	7	8	9	10
11	12	13	14	15	16	17
18	19	20	21	22	23	24
25	26	27	28	29	30	31

Old Ranch

One day a citrus ranch was put up for sale. Its owners bought a new property and moved all their belongings there. The former peacock cages also stood empty and silent. It had wire mesh for the birds' safety. The active housewife Allen, who loved to add unexpected twists to her life, decided to embark on a new adventure. Her personality was filled with love and care for all living things. She loved creating beauty around her, and wanted to fill the silent garden with the pleasant energy of the pets wandering around.

***

February 2026

February, 2026 *"May chickens come cheeping?"*

Sun	Mon	Tue	Wed	Thu	Fri	Sat
1	2	3	4	5	6	7
8	9	10	11	12	13	14
15	16	17	18	19	20	21
22	23	24	25	26	27	28

***

New Residents

One day Allen stopped by the village store, selected two hens, placed them in a cardboard box, and carried them to her car.

The German shepherd Tuzik was waiting in the backseat. The dog was Allen's faithful companion on all her trips. The appearance of something alive and softly squeaking in the ca alarmed the loving dog. Tuzik immediately sniffed the box of chickens, intending to have a snack. But he was immediately restrained by the stern voice of his beloved owner.

- Why had she taken me along for such an unusual purchase, if the dog couldn't enjoy such delicious-smelling little birds?

- Unpleasantly thought Tuzik.

Upon arriving to the ranch, Allen put young hens in the former peacock cage. A nutritious dinner was waiting for the hens inside it. The sweet little birds felt very pleasant in this new home. There was no more a fierce struggle for the food bowl. Finally, they dined without rivalry or constant jabs of their more aggressive sisters. And then, they settled down to sleep in the farthest corner of the cage, tenderly embracing for warmth and comfort. At this evening devoted Tuzik got a delicious bone, and licked it gratefully.

***

March 2026

March, 2026

"Curses, like chickens, always come home to roost"

Sun	Mon	Tue	Wed	Thu	Fri	Sat
1	2	3	4	5	6	7
8	9	10	11	12	13	14
15	16	17	18	19	20	21
22	23	24	25	26	27	28
29	30	31				

***

Competition

The next day, the owner decided the hens would feel safer with a protector, a rooster. She called the special farm where she'd once bought her peacocks. The farm owner immediately brought her a two-year-old, very handsome rooster. Peter the Rooster boldly entered the chicken coops, enclosed by wire mesh. At first, he thought he'd have to compete with the other roosters for dominance again. But suddenly, he discovered that there were no roosters in the coops, only two very young hens. The rooster was overjoyed and crowed joyfully: "Finally, my dream has come true, and I have my own home! Not just a house, but a palace, a real kingdom. What a miracle, no rivals, only my own hens."

***

April 2026

April, 2026

"The raven sees its chickens as falcons"

Sun	Mon	Tue	Wed	Thu	Fri	Sat
			1	2	3	4
5	6	7	8	9	10	11
12	13	14	15	16	17	18
19	20	21	22	23	24	25
26	27	28	29	30		

***

The hens in the coop also immediately perked up and became much happier.

-"Oh, he is a handsome fellow! I will be his most beloved companion," - said the larger hen Galina.

"No, I will be his best friend"- said another hen Katia.

She hopped up to the rooster and perched very close to him. Then she began following him everywhere, side by side. But Peter the Rooster said to them: "You all will be my favorite hens". But when he would fly up to a perch somewhere, Katia would follow him there. The hens began to compete for the rooster's attention, and strong Galina, at every opportunity, began pecking at Katia's tail.

Soon, the owner noticed that Katya had developed a bare skin near her tail. Allen became very concerned and decided to help her. She bought a special medicine and sprayed chicken's tail, disguising the plucked area.

***

May 2026

May, 2026

"Priests, friars, nuns, and chickens never have enough"

Sun	Mon	Tue	Wed	Thu	Fri	Sat
					1	2
3	4	5	6	7	8	9
10	11	12	13	14	15	16
17	18	19	20	21	22	23
24	25	26	27	28	29	30
31						

***

Hard Working Rooster

At any time of the day, Peter the Rooster had a lot of work to do. Therefore, in the morning, he preferred to dress up and professionally. He was wearing a light shirt with black polka dots and black pants. Only his magnificent tail, with its dark green feathers, shimmered mysteriously in the sun. Peter's attractive plumage captured the imagination of simple-minded hens.

But most importantly for everyone was that the smart Rooster had excellent past experience. He was brought a place where there were many similar roosters, and all fought each other for dominance. There, in the old place, only people helped him avoid serious trouble. This is why the grateful Rooster treasured this good memory about people and was not aggressive towards them.

In the new place, he really liked the young, still completely inexperienced hens. He was delighted that now he alone would have power and authority there. He dreamed of expressing his desire to care for, protect, and love these young hens. But most importantly, he wanted to teach them all the wisdom of life.

From February to May, it was mating season for all the roosters. Ideally, each rooster needed twelve hens for a heavenly life. Only then would peace and order reign in the hen family.

Soon, every hen was trying to please him, sitting next to him, pecking at his sides, and seemingly preening his feathers. Every day, Peter the Rooster would single out a particular hen for special attention and teach her something important about life.

However, the most importantly, the clever little Rooster made sure everyone received his attention equally. He intuitively understood that peace and joy were the most important things in any family.

Even more important was building each hen's confidence in his care and love. He personally maintained order, discipline, and a strict hierarchy in his family. Therefore, Rooster was loved by everyone and remained the head and leader in all situations.

***

June 2026

June, 2026

"The hen's eyes are with her chickens".

Sun	Mon	Tue	Wed	Thu	Fri	Sat
	1	2	3	4	5	6
7	8	9	10	11	12	13
14	15	16	17	18	19	20
21	22	23	24	25	26	27
28	29	30				

***

Growing Family

Allen usually was quick to make decisions and persistent in achieving any goal. Without thinking twice, one day in April she went back to the village store, and chose five more red hens. The hens were still teenagers, and they hadn't yet grown combs and wattles.

Allen knew that they would begin laying eggs, when they will be five months old. The Rooster Peter, seeing five more new hens, was overjoyed by this pleasant surprise. He felt like the king of the world, at least in his flock now of seven. All the hens quickly recognized his passionate nature. They learned that the rooster is getting to attack after he was flapping his wings and fluffing up his feathers around his neck.

Within two days, everyone had settled into their new surroundings. And on the third day, the owner let them all out of the coop into the fenced garden.

Peter the Rooster was trying to show that he was the smartest one there, and everyone should love him. He gallantly let the hens out of the coop, reminding them of the importance of obeying him — the head of the household. Then, his proud, unhurried demeanor emphasized that he was the one making all the decisions. Peter the Rooster usually was quietly grumbling at his mistress for the interfering in his family business.

***

July 2026

July, 2026 *Don't count your chickens before they are hatched"*

Sun	Mon	Tue	Wed	Thu	Fri	Sat
			1	2	3	4
5	6	7	8	9	10	11
12	13	14	15	16	17	18
19	20	21	22	23	24	25
26	27	28	29	30	31	

August 2026

August, 2026

"It may be the rooster that does all the crowing, but it's the hen that delivers the goods

Sun	Mon	Tue	Wed	Thu	Fri	Sat
						1
2	3	4	5	6	7	8
9	10	11	12	13	14	15
16	17	18	19	20	21	22
23	24	25	26	27	28	29
30	31					

***

Magic Garden

Every morning, first, the chicken family goes to the feeder, and then to the gate to the garden. At this time, some hens are quietly and tenderly singing their joyful songs, anticipating a pleasant stroll.

When Allen opens the door to the coop, the hens quickly run up the hill and begin grazing on the green grass.

In the garden, Peter the Rooster first looks around for any signs of danger. He turns his head in all directions, constantly guards his family, and even is looking up at the sky, where a hawk might fly.

***

September 2026

September, 2026

"When you can't get meat, chickens and bacon are good"

Sun	Mon	Tue	Wed	Thu	Fri	Sat
		1	2	3	4	5
6	7	8	9	10	11	12
13	14	15	16	17	18	19
20	21	22	23	24	25	26
27	28	29	30			

***

The hens are very happy to find themselves in the wonderful world of the garden. It is their entertainment, a place for exercise, learning, and adventure. While wandering through the garden, the hens search for small stones and swallow them for better digestion.

Peter the Rooster is teaching each of them how to properly dig in the soil, looking for worms or other tasty and necessary things. He makes special sounds while doing this. If Peter senses the danger or decides they've had enough of their walk, he makes a special sound, calling everyone home. He is the last one to enter the coop, to make sure that everyone is backing home.

Peter generally tries to be in control, and he likes to communicate with the hens on various topics. He himself eats little, and only when he's sure his entire family is eaten and full.

But one day, Peter the Rooster suddenly flapped his wings and cried loudly:

- "Danger! - A dog is behind the fence!""

The hens perked up and raised their heads, looking around. This is how Peter the Rooster taught them to pay attention to his warnings. But when a real and imminent danger approached, the whole flock screamed loudly, the chickens cluck and Peter screamed loudly. Then, the owner would come out and look around, how to help her chickens.

***

October 2026

October, 2026 *"Chickens are counted in autumr*

Sun	Mon	Tue	Wed	Thu	Fri	Sat
				1	2	3
4	5	6	7	8	9	10
11	12	13	14	15	16	17
18	19	20	21	22	23	24
25	26	27	28	29	30	31

***

Novermber 2026

November, 2026

Laughter is good both for the body and for the soul and helps us to remain positive

Sun	Mon	Tue	Wed	Thu	Fri	Sat
1	2	3	4	5	6	7
8	9	10	11	12	13	14
15	16	17	18	19	20	21
22	23	24	25	26	27	28
29	30					

***

Wonderful Morning

For all the ranch residents being in the garden was the greatest pleasure. Peter the Rooster cared for his hens with all the depth of his heart. When he saw his mistress approaching, he began his usual quiet muttering. And the hens, seeing their mistress with bread in her hands, ran to her. The mistress would perch on a stump and extend her hand to them.

The hens adored the pieces of bread, and standing very close to their mistress, they would try to snatch them from her hands. And the others would quietly sing their tender songs, expressing their delight at such a wonderful life.

December 2026

December, 2026

Laughter gives us the opportunity to see everything in perspective.

Sun	Mon	Tue	Wed	Thu	Fri	Sat
		1	2	3	4	5
6	7	8	9	10	11	12
13	14	15	16	17	18	19
20	21	22	23	24	25	26
27	28	29	30	31		

***

The ranch owner placed fresh water and several plates with various delicious foods under the olive tree. She added a few crushed oyster shells to the variety of grains to replenish calcium and build strong eggshells.

A few of the hungriest hens ate whatever the housewife placed before them. The others, however, adored gathering green grass first. But Peter ate quickly, because his main concern was making sure all his hens were well-fed. After feeding, Peter led his family on a tour of the garden, and they delightedly explored everything around them.

One day, Peter discovered a huge pile of wood chips under the Bougainvillea bush. That beautiful bush was climbing up on the oak tree. Rooster led his family there, and for several hours, they delightedly rummaged around, turning everything upside down and digging up something tasty.

Sometimes, small birds would fly in and rummage through the wood chips, as if mocking and mimicking the naive hens. Under the constant watchful eye of Peter the Rooster, this wonderful pile of wood chips became the hens' favorite pastime.

***

Squirrels and Hawks

The hens had a fenced garden, where they soon ate all the grass and dug up all the soil. But anyway, every day, the hens would roll around in much-needed dust, taking a mud bath. This was good for their feathers and bodies, cleansing them of parasites.

When it was time to change their roosting area or send them back into the coop, the owner would take a hose and spray water behind the chickens. The hens disliked being wet and would quickly run to the right place.

But one day, at sunset, the owner noticed one hen missing from the coop and went looking for her. The huge daisies bushes grew near a tall oak tree. They created a safe shelter where the hens could wait out any danger coming from above.

The owner discovered Katya the hen, peacefully resting there. The weakest and seemingly least intelligent hen had the instinct to sit in hiding, holding her breath, amid the shrill cries of a hunting hawk. When Katya the hen heard the voice of her owner, who always protected her from the other hens, she crawled out from under the bushes and ran into the coop.

- "Or maybe she was looking for a secluded spot to lay eggs. All the hens were already ready to reproduce," - the owner thought.

But besides the hawk, there was another nuisance in the coop. These were thieving squirrels. Upon seeing the squirrels, Peter would begin to cry anxiously, calling for his owner's help. At such moments, all the hens would scurry about excitedly, trying to fight off the uninvited intruders. They flapped their wings, screamed angrily and clucked to get rid of the intruders. But some young, mischievous squirrels often didn't even react to the chicken family's outrage. They simply chased each other, teasing the hens.

For several days in a row, the owner watched in despair as several squirrels came into the huge chicken coop with an open door, ran around, playing and ate the chicken food.

The main danger of this invasion was that squirrels, like mice, carried dirt and germs. Then the owner noticed that the hens had begun scratching their heads.

So, a few days later, she bought special metal traps. The squirrels would get inside the trap through two small open doors to get the sunflower seeds. Then the doors slammed shut, and the squirrels realized that they were trapped.

The hens were very surprised to find this trap with squirrels inside. This became their main entertainment for a while. They crowded around the cage, watching what the squirrels would do and how they would try to escape. The hens lightly pecked at the thieves, daring them to quickly escape.

Some of the hens, having flown to the top bars of the coop, occupied these privileged positions, and watched everything.

And the all-knowing rooster, Peter, never missed an opportunity to teach even the squirrels a lesson, emphasizing his importance in the life of the coop. - "Well, foreigners, are you trapped in a cage?"

And then he turned to his family: "Look, hens, how to defend your home!" - Peter retreated to the wall, took a running start, and, flapping his wings menacingly, rushed toward the squirrel cage.

"Anyone who comes into our house with a sword will perish by the sword!"- He used an old proverb.

Although the trap was large and the squirrels were safe, they couldn't escape. Then, the owner took them away from the chicken coop and set them free. The squirrels were glad to be free and never returned to the coop.

***

First Eggs

When the hens were seven months old, they began dreaming of children or chicks. Their owner created a special place for it in the coop.

One morning, one hen woke up and dropped her first egg down from the top perch, where she slept. The egg wasn't quite strong enough yet and broke. Another hen joyfully ran to the egg and pecked it.

After that, all the hens began searching everywhere for secluded spots for their most important role in life. First, they tried to find a safe spot somewhere in the garden and hide their eggs there for the future offspring.

Another hen found a safe spot under a small child's chair against the wall of the house. She laid her first egg there and didn't want to return to the coop. She sat on the egg for a long time, dreaming of her firstborn chick hatching. But the owner found the spot and tried to return the hen to the coop.

For a while, the other hens also tried to lay their eggs in different places in the garden. Seeing this, the owner told Peter the Rooster that it was time to intervene and teach his hens to lay their eggs in a specific spot in the coop. Peter quickly understood this, and felt that he should help his hens in that job.

Soon, he led his entire family into the coop, lined them up in front, and began teaching his hens to lay their eggs in the right place.

He climbed into a special box with hay that his mistress provided for them. There he began twirling and turning, showing the hens that this was an excellent nest for laying eggs. He explained again and again that this is the most convenient and safe spot for their main activity – laying eggs. All seven hens stood before him, watching his explanation.

Then the Rooster emerged and said:

- "Now you will come here one by one and do your main task."

But for a while, several hens, not having learned this lesson well, wandered around the garden still looking for a place to lay their eggs. Then, the mistress placed artificial eggs in their coop to convince them of the correct place for their work. The next morning, the mistress found several small brown eggs in the correct spot indicated by the Rooster.

Then, two hens were especially stubborn in their desire to have chicks. They sat on the artificial eggs for days, surprised that there was no visible progress. Then the owner realized her mistake and removed the artificial eggs. But the hens continued to sit there, not leaving the nest to drink or eat. Allen had to give them a cold bath and move them to another part of the coop for a day. She wasn't ready for the expansion of the chicken family.

After this incident, the hens decided not to lay eggs at all for several days. The owner was upset and decided to change everything in the coop. She placed the artificial eggs in a new part of the coop. Soon, the curious hens noticed this and called the Rooster for help.

- "Don't worry, my dears," said Peter the Rooster. - "I'll help to check everything!" He approached the new spot and, craning his neck, examined the artificial eggs. Then, as always, he crawled into this secluded spot and began to squirm around.

The new spot under the chair was well-hidden, seemed secure, and there was some straw in it. The Rooster found nothing dangerous there, and the new spot was approved by him. The hens sang their sweet songs again and began to hatch their eggs in the new spot. Peter the Rooster was very smart and caring.

***

At first, the young hens laid small eggs without any problems. But one hen was pacing the garden and suffered. Then, she was sitting in a special spot for a long time and tried to squeeze the egg out. But the egg was too big.

Some other chicken owners suggested that a person would try to push the egg out of the hen with her own hands. But in this chicken coop was Peter, an unusually smart and caring Rooster. The hen complained to him about this problem. Seeing that, the smart and kind Peter the Rooster, approached the hen's nest and said again:

- "Don't worry, I'll help you!"

He jumped on her back and began pushing her sides, helping her squeeze the egg out. And after that, his beloved hen, Galina, began laying huge double-yolk eggs for several days.

"Poor girl!" - Allen thought - "And how wonderful that the caring and kind Rooster helps his hens. It is an amazing world of nature."

***

Hero

Peter the Rooster clearly saw his purpose in life and pursued it with devotion. At the slightest sign of danger, he would make a loud, peculiar sound, and the weakest hens would run closer to him. This usually happened when dogs appeared outside their fence.

One day, his owner forgot to move the elderly shepherd, Sonya, to another part of the garden. The hens, unsuspecting, were peacefully wandering around, pecking at something in the vegetable garden. Sonya, surprised by this unexpected intrusion into her garden, gathered her old strength and rushed toward the hens.

But the rooster was on guard. He puffed himself up, his neck feathers standing on end. Peter flapped his wings and cried loudly:

"Everyone! Run to the chicken coop! - Quickly!"

He literally kicked up a dust storm in front of the stunned old dog.

"Don't come near! I'll protect my hens to my last breath and my last feather!"

The old dog Sonya, although surprised by such a cocky bird, was a shepherd and not one to be timid. Besides, she already had huge experience fighting garden enemies. Sonya thought for a moment, looking at the seven bright brown birds darting around in panic before her. "Who should I catch first?" - She thought.

Meanwhile, the chickens had already scattered in different directions, and the smartest ones had even fled to the coop high spot.

And the Rooster loudly screamed at Sonya and menacingly flapped his wings. But for greater safety, he flew up to the roof. From there, Peter continued to loudly protest the violation of his chicken family's vital rights.

Allen came running at the unexpected noise and commotion in the garden. She saw Peter the Rooster, panicked and nervously pacing the high roof of the chicken coop, searching for a way into his home.

The owner led the surprised dog Sonya into the other side of the yard. Then she began calmly talk to Peter, helping him figure out the best way to get down. But the usually intelligent Rooster, in such an incredibly stressful situation, couldn't immediately figure out how to go down. Then the owner took the hose and began to water behind Peter, which prompted him to fly down. Then, as if nothing had happened, Peter walked slowly inside the coop, maintaining his dignity. The loving hens greeted their hero with joyful clucking.

The evening ended, as always, with an orderly arrangement of the chickens on the slats of the coop. The hens washed their feathers there, and then the Rooster flew up to them, getting ready to spend there their night. His favorite hens hugged him, laid their heads on him, and fell peacefully asleep.

***

The Rooster's Sounds

Every morning, shortly before dawn, the Rooster announced the arrival of a new day. And at sunset, he gathered his entire family in the coop and announced bedtime.

The Rooster constantly watched over his chicken family, walking proudly and leisurely, with his head held high. Another important task for the Rooster was protecting and feeding his hens. He taught them everything he knew. In the garden, Peter the Rooster would call the family to dig the earth, first showing them how to do it and how to find some protein food - worms. But most importantly, he dreamed of his chicks, every day making special effort to achieve this.

His main characteristic was his desire to communicate with everybody. He grumbled endlessly, at everything around him, constantly explaining and clarifying something to the hens. And when another hen rushes to the roost to hatch her eggs, the Rooster calls everyone to silence and respect.

And then, when an egg hatches, he flies high up on the crossbar, from where he can see the entire world, and declare it. The Rooster flaps his wings, loudly and joyfully proclaiming to the entire neighborhood the arrival of his future heir. The Rooster is very sensitive and responds at all events in the environment. Nothing goes without his loud crows and announcements.

***

The dogs near the porch in another part of the yard always barked hysterically, revealing the unwelcome arrival of coyotes, which roamed the ranch in packs. And Peter the Rooster immediately echoed them with a piercing cry. And then the hens supported their master with their own loud sounds. Several times a day, Peter the Rooster exchanges the latest news with his neighbor, who lives far beyond the vast orange groves.

Shortly before sunset, Peter the Rooster makes a special "cock-a-doodle-doo" call to gather his family and return them to the coop. That how the life on the ranch was going on...

***

Book 2. The Big Rooster

Seventy years earlier

***

Little Chicks

Long time ago, a little girl Allen lived in her grandmother's Anna and grandfather Minai. He was a former military man, and some people called him "Gorenych" for his cold and uncaring heart.

One day, just before the Easter, grandfather Minai gave his wife some money to go to the market. The food market was in the center of the town and Allen usually enjoyed going there with her grandmother. It was like an adventure trip near the lovely sea.

But one day grandmother Anna left the girl at home. That spring was not very warm, and the girl did not have a coat to go out, and no boots to run in the rain. Her old shoes had holes in the soles and she outgrew her old summer dress. Soon grandmother came back with a huge box and put it on the floor by the old stove.

Allen thought that maybe grandmother brought her some gifts in the big box. So the girl ran to the box and looked inside. However, there were tiny chickens that squeaked and moved on the bottom of the box. Apparently, they all had different parents, so they all looked like a cheerful rainbow. There were yellow chickens, brown and even multi-colored little chickens.

The wise Grandmother Anna chooses the biggest chick and put the blue ink on his wings:

- We will see who will grow up with these one: a hen or a rooster. But for now, you have to use very slow movements inside their box in order not to frighten them.

On the fourth day, you will let the chicks eat from your hand. Then, on day seven you could try to hold a new chick.

When the time is right, pick them up just a few inches from the ground or if they seem skittish, delay another day or two."

Then, the curious cat Murka ran up, sniffed the box, licked her lips and thought: - "I wish I could eat a fresh chick now!"

But the cat Murka was smart; she did not want to get into any trouble. So, she did not touch the chickens when everybody was looking at her. Besides, the little girl Allen saw the hangry cat Murka, and gave her a little piece of bread and some milk, that she kept from own dinner. Murka happily accepted the food from the loving girl. Then, she came up and rubbed against Allen legs, quietly purring.

Then, hearing the cheerful commotion, suddenly, strict grandfather Minai came out of his room and said: - I'll have some great chicken soup in the summer!

But the kind grandmother Anna answered: -"We will raise these chickens, and they will give us fresh eggs every day. That will be your food. Also, I will sell some eggs to buy new clothes for my granddaughter Allen!"

Hearing this, Allen was delighted and began to wait for the chicks to grow up and lay such precious eggs. Grandmother put some water next to the chicks and fed them several boiled eggs from the old hens in the yard.

When seven days passed, Allen was allowed to hold one chicken. But with the first movement inside the box, all chicken got alarmed and nervous, and ran away from her. But grandmother was teaching that the girl first should drop her hand into a box slowly. Then, the chicks will get used to her smell, and then she could gently take one chick out and pat him.

***

***

Fun Garden

The beautiful garden was behind the grandmother's house with many fruit trees, bushes, and flowers. During the spring and summer, they brought delicious fragrance around. That incredible aroma was calming to Allen, little girl, giving her joy in life.

Also, little girl Alla often saw between the trees the bright light shining down and shimmering in different colors. That pleasant light gave her a confident feeling of future happiness.

When it became warmer, all the grown-up chickens were carried out into the garden. The grandmother fenced off a part of the garden with a metal net and the chickens walked there in good weather. And when it rained, they all were hidden in the chicken coop.

In warm sunny weather, little Allen ran to the magical garden, where she felt completely safe. In this enchanted land of flowers and fruits, insects and various small creatures, she remained for many hours, hiding from all troubles. In the fairy garden Allen watched living creatures, learned to understand their language and their thirst for life.

Once a while, suddenly, a black fast snake-viper, a symbol of death, appeared there. At such moments, everyone froze for a second, but then the happy life in the beautiful garden revived and bustles again.

In that garden of Allen childhood, many wonderful creatures lived merrily together, in harmony with nature. All of them were friends with Allen and taught her to overcome all obstacles on the way to her dreams. The Living Soul of the garden loved, caressed and protected the lonely girl. There, in an overgrown garden, sitting under the fragrant bushes and among flowers, a little girl dreamed of her future beautiful life. And then she left the garden with a sense of relief and renewal, full of new strength, with a new desire to love everything around.

***

Cat Murka Tales

Of course, the loving, wise cat Murka always accompanied the girl and ran nearby. The cat Murka loved her freedom, was independent, and was not afraid of anything. Long ago, in her feline childhood, Murka did not live in Grandma's house. When she was a small kitten, she lived in the wild forest. There, in order to survive, kittens learned to overcome any fear and catch mice for a dinner.

One day Murka was taken into the house, and she immediately started to care for little Allen. The cat slept with her on the top of the old fashioned stove, and told her different tales, comforting little girl in various troubles. Also, the cat Murka always accompanied the little girl everywhere, guarding and protecting her against all sorts of troubles and fears.

Sometimes Murka told her: -"If you feel that Fear is creeping closer and closer to you, tell yourself that you are not afraid of it. You should repeat it until Fear would run away. The Fear cannot fight courageous girls and will disappear. "

During some nights with the full moon, Allen was a sleepwalker. During her sleep, she walked to the dark garden, and cat Murka ran next to Allen, repeating: "Do not be afraid of anything! I am here to protect you. I will bite anyone who dares to harm you."

One night, Allen went to the garden with the caring cat to see where Fear lived. But they did not find anything terrible there. Then, they returned home and went to sleep again. At that night, the Allen's Soul was resting and rejoicing. It grew up and became stronger.

***

One Moon to Love

Once before Christmas, while watching lonely Allen, the cat Murka told her about how once she was a loving mother. But right after the birth of all her kittens, Gorenych took them all in an unknown direction. After that, the mother Murka never saw her kittens again and was missing them terribly.

This why the kind cat Murka tried to reassure the little girl in her love and whispered:

- Sleep, little babe, and I will sing you a comforting tale. Once upon a time, one a furry cat was wandering around the garden. And a horned goat walks after the cat. They had a good friendship, because they cared for each other...

When a good weather comes back, I'll bring you to the magic garden. And the fabulous Moon will help us to learn many new secrets. After all, we all have only one moon. This moon shines for all birds and animals, for all-all people on the Earth. We need to love our one Moon. Meow - meow". And Allen felt asleep....

Cats always purr with people, but they don't purr with each other. They believe that their purr is the ideal language for humans to speak with. Therefore, they humble themselves before people, telling children fairy tales, and sometimes fulfilling their dreams.

But some people understand the language of their cats, as Allen understood her cat Murka. With the stories and consolations of her cat, the girl fell fast and sweetly asleep.

And in a dream, heroes of wonderful fairy tales came to her again; especially fairy tales who loved to visit her before Christmas.

***

Tamed Hens

When it became quite warm, a large family of chickens and a big Rooster settled in the chicken coop. Every day they went out for a walk in the fresh air. But the young chicks stayed only in a fenced place. Grandmother looked at the chick whose feathers had been painted with ink and said:

"Look! There was a big chick that now became a rooster. But we need to have only one rooster in the coop. Otherwise, it will be constant fight for the dominance."

The chicken house (coop) was in the barn, where the grandfather built several shelves for them to sit. Then, caring grandmother put some hay there for the hens' comfort. The hens laid eggs there, dreaming of raising new chicks.

During the day, the hens walked everywhere and collected everything edible from the ground, usually all kinds of the plant seeds. They dug up the whole garden, looking for worms. And the grandmother used to say: "Give the chicken a garden bed, but the whole garden would not be enough for her."

In the evening, grandmother went out into the garden with a bag of different grains. She called for the chickens (chip-chip-chip), and threw them the seeds of wheat or corn. The hens rushed to her and screamed:

"Oh, run faster, faster! The sun is going down! We must have time to eat, and then run to our shelter to lay eggs."

The grandmother's chickens lived a good life. They slept in a warm coop, and were spending their days roaming the garden, foraging to their hearts' content. Happy chickens were active, while scratching around in the grass, lying in the sun, or taking a bath in the dirt.

Chickens recognized many faces around them, and knew grandmother well because she fed them. They were following her in the yard just before the time to have dinner. Sometimes, the grandmother gave some rich in fat diet to several hens, and then they produced more flavorful eggs. Many hens displayed some affection to grandmother by rubbing their heads against her legs.

The grandmother was petting them, and hens were showing their friendliness back. Also, she told little Allen to come to chickens calmly and interact with them gently. Only with some calmness and care, chickens allowed Allen to pet them.

Grandmother Anna was teaching her granddaughter:

-"If you want chickens or other live creatures or people like you, you have to spend quality time with them. For example, before feeding them, announce: 'Dinner is served!'

Remember that for every action there is a reaction. When you go to the chickens, try to look nice and smile, bring them some treats. They love the hand that feeds them."

Chickens always remember positive and negative experiences and connect it with the faces. They recognize and pass that information on to all members of their family.

They all were afraid of the grandfather Minai (Gorenych), especially when he had an axe in his hands. At such sad moments, all hens expressed anxiety and tried to hide in the coop. They knew that one of them is going for the dinner.

***

King Rooster

There was only one big Rooster among the hens in the yard. There was no place for the other roosters. When the new chicken-boys grew up, they were fighting too much with each other, and wanted to compete with the main Rooster.

But the main Rooster wanted to be the only King. He did not want to have any competition. Therefore, most of the new chicken-boys often were sent to the soup. But the grandfather Minai kept one rooster for the yard to guard it.

This one Rooster was huge, strong, colorful and very handsome. But he had a big ego, and acted slightly too selfish, which was not very good for all others.

At sunset Grandmother poured some grain for all hens. But this Rooster was the first to have dinner. No one dared to eat grain near him before he would be full. Also, this rooster fluttered his colorful wings, and was not in a hurry to come to the grandmother. When he was already full, then the hens could also eat.

This Rooster was the master of the yard, and insisted that all consider him as a King of the Yard. It looked like the grandmother encouraged his selfishness, and gave him a respectful name "Peter Petrovich". For the dinner she called him loudly:

- "Peter-Petrovich! Come to eat, and come I will pat you!"

Grandmother stroked the Rooster on his comb and neck, which he really liked. Then the Rooster sulked with importance, spread his wings and feathers, and became completely tame. But he allowed only grandmother to do this with him and did not trust anyone else.

The Rooster kept a distance from other. So, everybody understood his importance and respected his independence. The Rooster felt that he was a very special person, important and very handsome bird. He forced all chickens to call him respectfully “Peter- Petrovich”. The hens followed his rules, not daring to disobey. Many other living creatures, including Allen, were slightly afraid of the wrath of the cocky Peter-Petrovich.

This huge Rooster was a pretty serious person. He could run after the girl or after any stranger dared to come in the gate of the yard. Peter-Petrovich painfully pinched such person if somebody was in his way to sovereignty.

In the morning he loved walking around the courtyard with an important look and listening to Allen sing: - “Rooster! Golden and silky head. Why do you get up so early and why do you sing so loudly? Let our little Allen girl to sleep some more.”

After this song, he became a little friendlier to the girl, and let her stroke him gently. And most importantly, the Rooster was sure that the famous Russian poet Alexander Pushkin had written about him and his ancestors in a fairy tale called "Rooster Golden Comb". Allen was very fond of Pushkin's fairy tales, especially that one.

Grandmother said that the Rooster has a tendency to “narcissism”. He looked and acted as any narcissistic person would act. Allen later asked her about who was Narcisse. One evening, before going to bed, the grandmother told Granddaughter an ancient legend.

***

Rosster - Narcisse

Grandmother Anna once said that the Rooster was spoiled and loved himself too much. She compared him to Narcisse, and told Allen an old tale.

“Once upon a time in Ancient Greece there were many Gods. And there lived a handsome young man named Narcissus. He was indifferent and cold to people. He was not interested in their opinions, and did not need anyone to be with him. He loved and constantly admired himself.

Once, one beautiful nymph fell in love with this young man. But he not only did not answer her with any emotions, but even ridiculed her being in love and did it in an offensive and rude form.

In those days, love was considered a great feeling, and mockery of it belonged to the category of the biggest sin.

Having learned about the insult by the laughter, the beautiful goddess Aphrodite decided to punish the handsome but egoist Narcissus. One hot day the young man was on the hunt. He wanted to drink water from a stream. But suddenly saw the face of a charming young person in it and fell in love with him.

Although his own reflection was looking at him, Narcissus could not take his eyes off the beautiful reflection. With wild passion, he fell to the surface of the water, wanting to kiss the reflection. He had neither the strength nor the desire to move away from the water.

In the end, his divine body disappeared, and at this place, a no less beautiful flower blossomed. This flower came to be called a daffodil. It became associated with deceptive desires and selfishness."

- "So, it looks like our big Rooster, Peter-Petrovich, is similar to this "Narcisse character" of an ancient legend," - added the Grandmother.

***

Rooster's Joy

The Rooster Peter-Petrovich had many reasons to feel so important and proud of all the work he was doing around the yard. The Rooster got up before everyone else and crowed loudly when it was still dark outside. Then Grandmother got up, started the smoking stove, and began to cook something on it, scolding "Gorenych"- her husband for his idleness. Allen woke up from the smoke of the stove, and hearing the Big Rooster voice:

- "Good morning! What a lovely day is coming!"

Also, The Rooster loved that his hens laid brown eggs. These eggs were not golden but still they were very valuable. The orange chickens had also some red feathers and hatched the brown eggs. They looked exactly like the Rooster, like two drops of water.

Peter-Petrovich has already risen more than one generation of chickens. But most of the boys went to the chicken soup, especially when somebody in the house was sick. Grandmother Anna told Allen that the chicken soup was a healthy food, helping with a fast recovering.

Peter-Petrovich knew it, and he was especially proud of this fact that he serves for the benefit of mankind. But once he was scared and tried to fly over the fence. However, Grandfather Minai saw it, got his ax and slightly cut the tips of the Rooster's wings. However, the Rooster still waved his wings, and crowed loudly while announcing: - "I am a very strong Rooster and can do anything I want."

But Grandmother Anna replied: - "Our Rooster is protecting us from all strangers who wish to enter the yard without permission. So, we will keep our Rooster healthy and happy. He will continue to warn us about the intruders"!

Rooster consoled his left hens in the chicken coop, saying that tomorrow the sun would rise again, and he would sing songs, and they would be fed with delicious grains. "So, we must enjoy life while there is a head on our shoulders," - said the Rooster, and the chickens faithfully believed him.

***

Cat Murka Wisdom

One day the cat Murka wanted to tell Allen a very important wisdom. She told a new fairy-tale, hinting at the gullibility and meager mind of the roosters.

"Once upon a time there lived a cat and a rooster in a small hut. The cat wandered through the woods looking for some food. And the rooster stayed at home and cooked dinner. Leaving, the cat strictly said to the rooster: -"Don't talk to strangers, don't trust their nice words, and don't accept any gifts from them!"

The cunning fox saw that the cat was not at home, ran to the hut, and sang under the window some flattering words: “Hi, handsome Rooster! Come out on the porch and sing to me! Your voice is so beautiful! I'll give you delicious chocolate for your song”.

The rooster believed the sweetly speaking fox and went out to sing to her. But the fox grabbed him and rushed back to the forest to eat him.

However, at that moment, the courageous cat was on the way back home and rescued the rooster. This is how the rooster remembered that he should not believe the gentle words of strangers.”

Rooster Peter-Petrovich heard what the cat Murka was talking about, and croaked in response: - "We are also smart and do not succumb to the temptations of strangers!" And then the Rooster reminded that he was a very useful bird because he was caring for the household.

***

Rooster’s Dreams

The old, big Rooster Peter-Petrovich dreamed that one day all his hens would try harder and start to lay the golden eggs. “I wish our grandmother would be delighted! She wouldn't need to work so much around the house. And the girl Allen would have new clothes,”- said the Rooster.

But the cat Murka objected to him: “But then the grandmother could not cook eggs for breakfast and feed the family. And we wouldn't have chicken soup, which is so necessary for all sick children".

Peter-Petrovich agreed with the cat Murka, but continued to dream. He was nevertheless proud that every day his hens laid although not golden eggs, but close to the golden color, the brown eggs. Then, from those brown eggs the orange-colored chickens appeared, looking exactly like Peter-Petrovich himself.

The Rooster was proud that after people ate the chicken soup, everyone quickly recovered. That fact was a special pride of the Rooster, because his chickens served for the benefit of humanity, providing everyone with chicken soup.

Also, the Rooster counted his pride, he worked hard every day, telling about the time, woke everyone up right on the clock. His ringing voice was followed by other roosters in the area. They shouted one after another: "It's time to get up and start work! Give us some food".

People loved the loud voice of the Rooster, announcing the time. They did not need to buy a watch.

The most important meaning of the Rooster's life was to protect the yard, garden and his chickens from any unknown guests. If he saw that someone unfamiliar approached the gate of the house, the Rooster immediately began to crow loudly and call Grandfather Minai to come out with an ax. If the uninvited guest nevertheless dared to enter the gate, then the Rooster immediately chased him menacingly, trying to peck and drive away.

The Rooster has proven in practice how useful and necessary it is for everyone in the yard to have him as a King of the Yard. So, the owners took care and pampered this Rooster, and Peter-Petrovich lived happily ever after.

***

About Author

Elena Pankey is a world traveler. She has more than forty years of job experience in the different areas of the performing art, cinema, theater and producing charity shows. After finishing her dance career, Elena began to write fun book about Argentine Tango dancing art, and her life adventures. All books written by Elena Pankey have fun, educational, and wise stories. Most of the books are telling about different garden creatures. She wrote about her dogs, cats, peacocks, chicken, and several fairy tales for children.

While living in CA, she continues to travel the world, teaching, dancing and writing.

***

Rights Reserved

***

ISBN: 978-1-952907-94-4

www.ingramcontent.com/pod-product-compliance
Lightning Source LLC
Chambersburg PA
CBHW071952190726
48293CB00004B/1447

* 9 7 8 1 9 5 2 9 0 7 9 4 4 *